Fossils
What Dinosaurs Left Behind

by Ruth Owen

Consultant:
Dougal Dixon, Paleontologist
Member of the Society of Vertebrate Paleontology
United Kingdom

New York, New York

Credits

Cover, © Zack Frank/Shutterstock and © Kim Steele/Getty Images; 2–3, © Gabbro/Alamy; 4, © Jason Love/Burke Museum; 5, © Herschel Hoffmeyer/Shutterstock; 6L, © aminkorea/Shutterstock; 6R, © Gabbro/Alamy; 7T, © sruilk/Shutterstock; 7B, © Kim Steele/Getty Images; 8–9, © Tom Connell; 10–11, © Tom Connell; 12–13, © Tom Connell; 14, © Kenneth Keifer/Shutterstock; 15, © Tom Connell; 16T, © Tom Connell; 16B, © Larry Shaffer/Black Hills Institute of Geological Research; 17, © Vlad G/Shutterstock; 18B, © Public Domain; 18–19, © James Kuether; 20, © Aaron Fredlund; 21, © Shinobu Ishigaki; 22T, © W. Scott McGill/Shutterstock; 22B, © Fotoluminate LLC/Shutterstock; 23T, © Breck P. Kent/Shutterstock and © Bjoern Wylezich/Shutterstock; 23B, © Pressmaster/Shutterstock.

Publisher: Kenn Goin
Senior Editor: Joyce Tavolacci
Creative Director: Spencer Brinker
Image Researcher: Ruth Owen Books

Library of Congress Cataloging-in-Publication Data

Names: Owen, Ruth, 1967– author.
Title: Fossils : what dinosaurs left behind / by Ruth Owen.
Description: New York, New York : Bearport Publishing, [2019] | Series: The
   dino-sphere | Includes bibliographical references
   and index.
Identifiers: LCCN 2018049817 (print) | LCCN 2018053172 (ebook) | ISBN
   9781642802535 (Ebook) | ISBN 9781642801842 (library)
Subjects: LCSH: Dinosaurs—Juvenile literature. | Fossils—Juvenile
   literature. | Reptiles, Fossil—Juvenile literature.
Classification: LCC QE861.5 (ebook) | LCC QE861.5 .O8457 2019 (print) | DDC
   560—dc23
LC record available at https://lccn.loc.gov/2018049817

For more information, write to Bearport Publishing Company, Inc., 45 West 21st Street, Suite 3B, New York, New York 10010. Printed in the United States of America.

10 9 8 7 6 5 4 3 2

Contents

Found!

One day, two **scientists** were walking in a **desert** in Montana.

Suddenly, they spotted some giant, brown bones in a rock.

bones

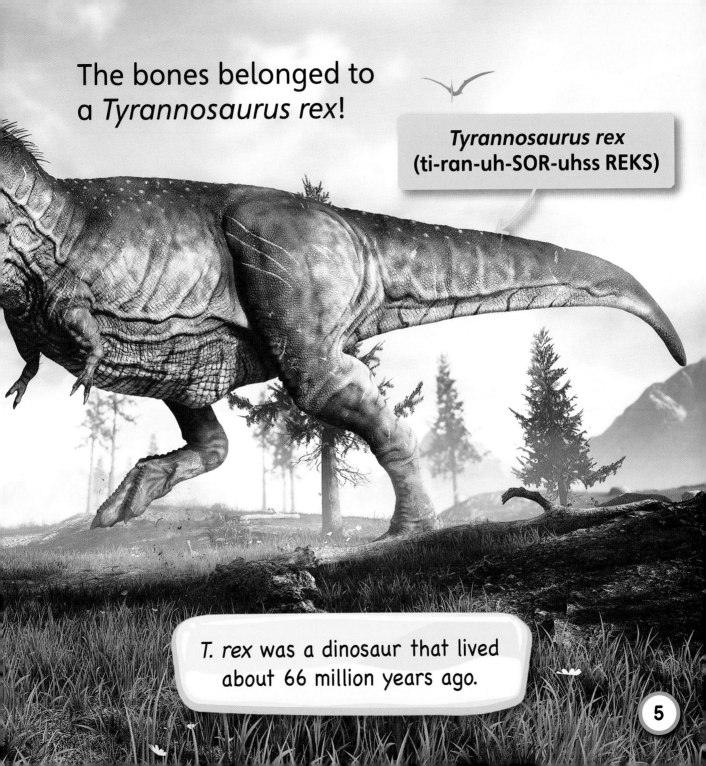

The bones belonged to
a *Tyrannosaurus rex*!

Tyrannosaurus rex
(ti-ran-uh-SOR-uhss REKS)

T. rex was a dinosaur that lived
about 66 million years ago.

Fossil Bones

The dinosaur bones are **fossils**.

When the dinosaur was alive, its bones were white and chalky.

Fossil bones are dark and very hard. Why?

Over a long time, they turned to rock!

fresh bones

T. rex foot fossil

A dinosaur's teeth also became fossils. *T. rex* had the biggest teeth of any known dinosaur.

T. rex teeth

Turning into Rock

How did the *T. rex*'s bones become rock?

It took millions of years.

First, the dinosaur died near a river.

Then, other animals ate the soft meaty parts of the *T. rex*'s body.

Like animals today, dinosaurs died because they were ill, hurt, or old.

Washed Away

Soon, all that was left of the *T. rex* was its bones.

One day, lots of rain fell.

The rainwater washed the remains into the river.

Some bones sank into the mud on the river's bottom.

Other *T. rex* bones were swept far down the river.

Rock Hard

Thousands of years passed.

The *T. rex* became buried under layers and layers of mud.

Then the river dried up, and the mud turned to rock.

The *T. rex*'s bones turned to rock, too.

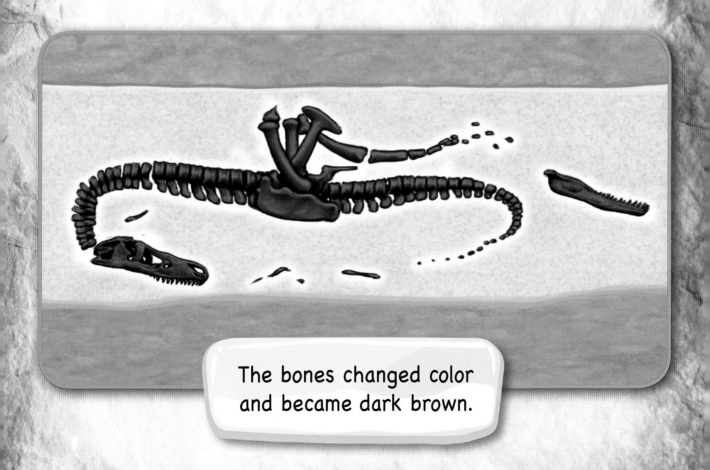

The bones changed color and became dark brown.

Dinosaur Mountain

Millions of years passed.

More rock formed and became a mountain with the *T. rex* inside.

Over time, the rocky mountain began to wear away.

Then, one day, scientists saw the *T. rex*'s bones poking from the rock!

How does a mountain wear away? Wind breaks off small pieces of it. Rain and melted snow also wash over rock, making it crumble.

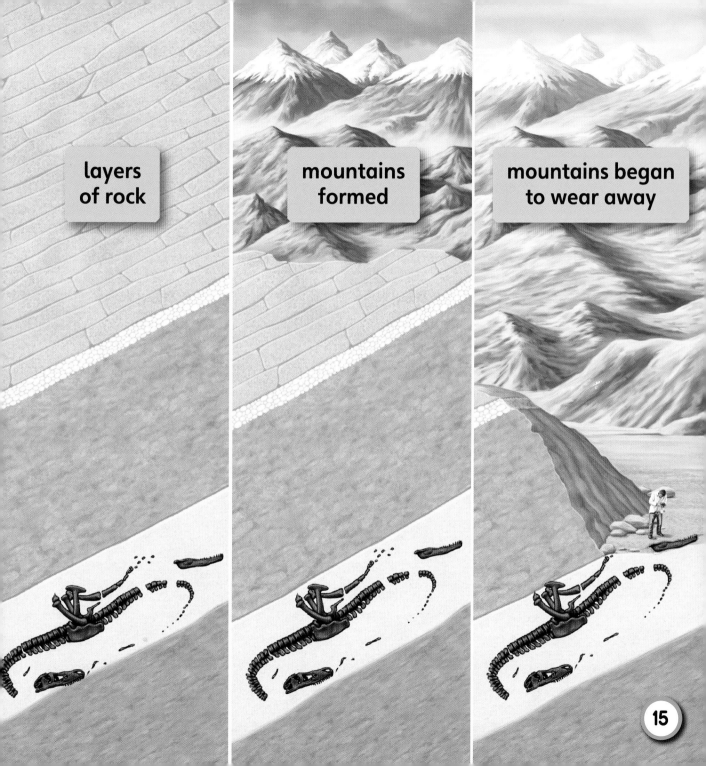

layers
of rock

mountains
formed

mountains began
to wear away

Prehistoric Puzzle

Once a fossil is found in a rock, scientists dig it out!

They work very carefully.

T. rex skin

Scientists have found fossils of dinosaur skin!

Scientists slowly uncover
pieces of a dinosaur.

Then, the fossils can be fitted
together like a jigsaw puzzle!

Fossil Poop

Dinosaurs didn't only leave behind bits of their bodies.

They also left behind poop!

A lump of fossil poop is called a **coprolite**.

coprolite

Scientists can find out what dinosaurs ate by looking at coprolites. It's even possible to see bits of plants or bones inside the poop!

Rocky Footprints

Dinosaurs also left behind footprints.

How?

a meat-eating dinosaur's footprint

A dinosaur stepped in mud.

Then the mud turned to rock.

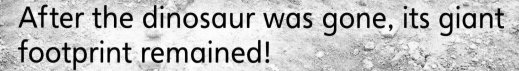

After the dinosaur was gone, its giant footprint remained!

One of the biggest footprints ever found was 3.5 feet (1 m) long. It belonged to a plant-eating dinosaur.

a plant-eating dinosaur's footprint

Glossary

coprolite (KOP-ruh-lite) the poop of an animal from long ago that has become a fossil

desert (DEZ-urt) dry land with few plants where very little rain falls

fossils (FOSS-uhlz)
the rocky remains of
animals and plants
that lived millions
of years ago

scientists
(SYE-uhn-tists)
people who
study nature
and the world

Index

Read More

Owen, Ruth. *Last Days of the Dinosaurs (The Dino-Sphere).* New York: Bearport (2019).

Peterson, Judy Monroe. *Fossil Finders: Paleontologists (Extreme Scientists).* New York: Rosen (2009).

Learn More Online

To learn more about dinosaurs, visit
www.bearportpublishing.com/dinosphere

About the Author

Ruth Owen has been developing and writing children's books for more than ten years. She first discovered dinosaurs when she was four years old—and loves them as much today as she did then!